MW01069323

How to Get FREE Government Grant Money for *Almost* Anything

Brought To You By:

Danielle Green

Table of Contents

<u>Legal Notice and Disclaimer:</u>

This book is for informational and entertainment purposes only. We've done our best to outline the process of finding "FREE" Grant Money and applying for it. In no way does the author or any associated parties guarantee that you will receive funding or anything all from these programs. Ultimately the decision of who receives any money in the form of a grant or assistance program is up to each individual entity.

Introduction

There's nothing more exciting than "FREE MONEY", and on the following pages you're going to learn how to get all the "FREE MONEY" you'll ever need!

The U.S. government alone gives out over $300 BILLION dollars in "FREE MONEY" and services every single year to American taxpayers. In addition, there are BILLIONS extra given away by private businesses and foundations. Any of this money could be rightfully yours; you just need to know where to find it and how to get it!

The good news is that there are grants and other sources of "FREE MONEY" for almost everything! Grants to pay bills, pay off debt, start a business, travel abroad, get a degree, train for a new job, invest in real estate, get legal help, and so much, much more...

Many of these programs simply don't advertise which is why you have never heard of them, until now. Or maybe you have heard of them, you just needed to know exactly how you can take advantage of them, and that's why you purchased this book.

Before we get started on how to get all of this "FREE MONEY", it helps if you have an understanding of what it is, where it comes from, and why it's given away.

WHERE DOES ALL THIS "FREE MONEY" COME FROM?

There are six major contributors to all the "FREE MONEY" you'll ever need:

*Federal Government
*State Government

*Local Government (city and county)
*Foundations
*Trusts
*Corporations

When you add up all of the contributors you're looking at over 20,000 Business Foundations, 24,000 State Programs, 30,000 Private Foundations, and 1,500 Federal Programs administered by 57 different Federal Agencies. These agencies administer BILLIONS of dollars to be given away each and every year. They need to give this "FREE MONEY" to someone. Why not you?

These foundations, programs, and agencies are responsible for giving away A LOT OF MONEY, but only to those of us that know how to APPLY for the money.

Once again, I can't stress this enough. The only people that have a chance to receive the money are those that apply for the money. The government does not advertise any of this information. So, if you want to take advantage of these programs you've got to be proactive and put in a little work - - **my goal is to make this work as simple and fast as possible.**

And this is why we are here today. We try to make this process as painless as possible, but (as with everything in life) sometimes it's simple and fast and sometimes it is not. Such is life! It may take you a week or it may take you 5 months to get a grant, but for most people it's worth it. After all, where else can you potentially receive $150,000 to open a restaurant? How about $15,000 to go back to school? Even $40,000 for a down payment on a house!

Are you starting to see how this works?

This may be the only place in the world where you have a chance to get money like this, and the truth is IT'S FUN! It is! Most people enjoy the process once they get comfortable with the various steps involved.

WHY WOULD THEY JUST GIVE AWAY ALL OF THIS MONEY?

Truthfully, there are hundreds, maybe even thousands of reasons this money is given away, but what's most important is that it's usually a win-win scenario.

For example, private foundation grants. These are given to small businesses, non-profits, and individuals by successful corporations or wealthy citizens and families, and they are FREE GRANTS.

Why would they do this? Private foundations are legally required to give away a certain percentage of their income every year. It's a net benefit for all parties involved. They get to keep their status as a non-profit organization, and grants are available to the public at large.

As you can imagine, for non-profit foundations this is a great way to promote good will and a sense of community. In return, they maintain their tax-exempt status, which is beneficial for them. This is just one example of why "FREE MONEY" is given away.

Keep in mind, our government is the largest source of "FREE MONEY" in the world today! Whether you take advantage of it or not – the money is there. Millions of people are entitled to this "FREE MONEY" and you can apply for as many programs as you want.

You are only limited by what you can do with the grant money and your imagination. So let your imagination run free while considering...

*Going to school
*Buying a franchise
*Manufacturing a product
*Marketing a service

*Perhaps you have an invention and you want a patent
*Expanding a business
*Renovating a home
*Buying a home
*Investing in real estate
*That you need money for your church

There are grants for EVERYTHING! Business needs, personal needs, the list is endless.

If you are eligible for any of this money, don't you want to know about it? Of course, you would, right? There is no limit to the number of grants that you can apply for. And you can go back again, and again, and again!

Think about it, every year 1,000,000 entrepreneurs get free grant money, contracts, and low interest loans from the government (and private companies looking to give away money). Many companies also run what they call "contests" which are also a great source of "FREE MONEY"! I used to think anyone that received these benefits had to be extremely rich or extremely poor. Little did I know that regular people just like you and me can tap into these government sources and benefit just like Ross Perot and George Bush did. If they can do it, we can do it!

But you have to APPLY! The steps in this book will help you with that process!

If there is a "trick" to any of this it is to have a realistic plan of action. Think of this process as something similar to the process of finding a new job. Apply, apply, and apply.

I think you and I would agree that most people understand the process of finding a "new job" takes a bit of work.

Most reasonable people expect to apply to multiple jobs/positions in order to find suitable work. No one seriously looking for employment applies to only one potential job/position, expects to go on one interview, and expects to be hired for that one job... right? Of course not! You must be realistic and have a plan "B" and apply for many possible job opportunities - and the same is true when applying for grants.

With grants you will qualify for some and you will not qualify for others! So you must apply, apply, apply and remember you can apply for as many grants as you want!

I've run into people that say you should not be taking money from these programs, and all I can really say is... I think you should. The money belongs to the taxpayers (you), the hardworking citizens of America (you)... so why shouldn't you apply and benefit from these grants.

It's ridiculous to think that these programs should only benefit the super rich or the super poor! For goodness sake, if you are the average hard-working American and you go to work every day to pay your bills... guess what? You deserve to apply for these programs just like everyone else!

If you were shopping for a pair of pants and you found something you wanted to buy being sold at a discount for 30% off and the sales associate forgot to give you the SALE PRICE... would you ask for the 30% discount? Of course you would! The discount is rightfully yours.

There are certain tax breaks in the tax code that people take advantage of every year... if you qualified for one of these tax breaks... would you take advantage of it? Of course you would! It's legal and you have every right to take certain tax breaks. Others are doing it, why not you?

Your tax dollars have been paying for these things. Isn't it time you reap some of these benefits? Maybe you are struggling to make ends meet. Maybe you're a struggling single parent. Maybe you are financially "fit" but could use a little assistance. It really doesn't matter. If you qualify for a particular grant, I believe you should take it. It's all there. You just need to find it and apply for it. It's not as tricky as many people believe.

READY FOR A FEW SAMPLE PROGRAMS?

GRANTS FOR BUYING A HOME

House for $1 plus Closing Costs -- This program is referred to as "Dollar Home Sales" and was created to help expand HUD's relationship with local government
http://www.hud.gov/offices/hsg/sfh/reo/goodn/dhmabout.cfm
$10,000 Down Payment Assistance -- American Dream Down Payment Initiative
http://www.hud.gov/offices/cpd/affordablehousing/programs/home/addi/index.cfm

$6,500 to Weatherize Your Home --
http://energy.gov/eere/wipo/weatherization-assistance-program

Thousands of non-profit organizations are all across the country. They have housing programs with counseling money, down payment money, and more. To find out about these programs contact: HUD approved housing counseling center –
http://www.hud.gov/offices/hsg/sfh/hcc/hcs.cfm
Call 800-569-4287 to find a local office near you.

GRANTS FOR MISCELLANEOUS EXPENSES

Need help with your energy bills? Winter or summer, see how to apply here -- http://www.acf.hhs.gov/programs/ocs/liheap/

$600-$900/Month to Pay The Bills -- Supplemental security income is cash to meet your basic needs: food, shelter, and clothing. Amounts are subject to change. http://www.ssa.gov/ssi

GRANTS FOR MEDICAL/FAMILY CARE EXPENSES

Prescription Drug Assistance -- http://www.pparx.org/

$10,000 to care for grandma and grandpa or other elderly family members? www.eldercare.gov

Assistance for hospital care? www.hrsa.gov

How about more affordable health insurance for kids? www.insurekidsnow.gov

GRANT RESOURCES

Would you like access to a database of federal programs available to local and state governments? https://www.cfda.gov/

COE is part of a partnership that distributes over $250 billion a year in grants! http://www.grantsolutions.gov

Are you eligible for a few dozen grants? http://www.benefits.gov/

Try http://foundationcenter.org On this site you can search four complete databases – grant makers, companies, grants, and 990 finder – to gather the most current information on $1.5 million in grants with over 96,000 funders.

GRANTS FOR EDUCATION/EDUCATORS

All federal programs for training and higher education are listed in the Catalog of Federal Domestic Assistance -- www.cfda.gov

Find the money you need for college. Easily search 2.7 million scholarships and grants --http://www.scholarships.com/

Find scholarships, internships, grants, and loans that match your educational profile. This database searches thousands of sources for nearly $3 Billion in aid! http://apps.collegeboard.com/cbsearch_ss/welcome.jsp?cleanup=yes –

Completed your degree? Want to continue? Grants are available -- http://www.grants.gov and http://www.aauw.org/fga/fellowships_grants

GRANTS TO STUDY OVERSEAS

Believe it or not there are ways to travel and you don't have to pay. Look into http://www.iie.org/en/Students and http://www.ed.gov/programs/iegpsflasf/index.html ...for scholarships/fellowships that provide funding for study abroad and in the states.

BIG MONEY FOR STARTING A BUSINESS

If you are looking to open a business of your very own, you are not alone. Small business grants and low interest loans are hot commodities - especially with people on a tight budget and with little access to start-up capital. However, there are HUNDREDS OF MILLIONS of dollars in "FREE MONEY" for entrepreneurs that know where to look...

Here are a few samples:

There are over 1000 small business development centers all over the US, and every year they help over half a million entrepreneurs at: www.sba.gov

Women in business! Find grant opportunities for women at:
http://www.womanowned.com,
 http://www.womensnet.net;
http://staff.lib.msu.edu/harris23/grants/3women.htm

The process of finding a small business grant program to apply for can be time consuming but also very rewarding. Make sure you have access to updated data streams or an easy way to navigate databases, and pay close attention to the eligibility criteria.

Eligibility can be based on your location, sales revenue, application date, number of years in business, sex, and race. When you begin your "grant-seeking-mission" and actively start searching there are some questions that you will want to consider. These include:

1. Do you have the time and the resources available so that you can search for a small business grant program and apply for it?

2. Can you afford to hire a consultant if you are unsure of (or don't have the time to) apply for grants properly? Or, can you learn the grant application process by yourself?

3. Does your business need the money right now for expansion, or can you wait for up to a year?

4. If you decide to personally apply for grants, do you have the time and resources to complete the process, which could include evaluation and reporting throughout the grant life-cycle?

If you want to take a look at small business grants available from the federal government, the best place to start is the Catalog of Federal Domestic Assistance (CFDA). *The CFDA lists thousands of grants from all government agencies for free*. Many business grants will be geared towards minority business development or rural business opportunity grants. Do not overlook the other assistance programs available such as equipment and training.

OTHER TYPES OF GRANT PROGRAMS

There are a good number of grants on the market today, and knowing which one to apply for will help you to choose the grant that you are most likely to get approved for.

While the types of grant programs available are vast, the following programs are most common:

Research and Development
Education
Career Development/Job Training
Disaster or Emergency Assistance
Community or Social Services
Project Grants
Small Businesses

As we've mentioned, a great place to start looking is on the federal level. http://Grants.gov lists all of the federal grants offered under a total of 21 categories. Review this list to find a category (or categories!) that match your grant seeking needs:
Agriculture
Arts
Business and Commerce
Community Development
Disaster Prevention and Relief
Education
Employment, Labor and Training
Energy
Environmental Quality
Food and Nutrition

Health
Housing
Humanities
Information and Statistics
Law, Justice and Legal Services
Natural Resources
Recovery Act
Regional Development
Science and Technology
Social Services and Income Security
Transportation

Search the categories that appeal to you to get information about various grant opportunities and their specific requirements. Remember that state and local government grants are available in these categories as well, so search out all opportunities nearest you!

Aside from government funding programs, there are several options for private funding. There are non-profit groups, which include faith-based centers and community initiatives, and there are foundations with a multitude of grant opportunities.

To give you an idea of the scale of grant funders that are out there, the following is a list of the Top 20 U.S. Foundations ranked by total giving. This list is provided by the Foundation Center: http://foundationcenter.org/findfunders/topfunders/top100giving.html

For organizational grant seekers, you will be searching opportunities available under these grant types:

General or Operating Support: To fund the general expenses or operating costs of your organization.

Program or Project Development Support: To fund specific projects (which likely fall under the categories listed above). This is where you will find the majority of competitive grants from all funding sources.

As a non-profit organization, the grant possibilities are unlimited. Search for opportunities in as many categories and from as many sources as possible!

Small Business owners will likely be searching for grants for starting or expanding a business, scientific research and development, or improving your business in some way – such as "going green" or training for new technologies. While there are plenty of federal grants available in the latter two categories, if you are starting a business you will likely want to gear your search toward private grant makers.

Now that you are more familiar with the types of grants available, we will move on to developing a grant proposal.

IMPORTANT FACTS ABOUT GRANTS AND FUNDING

Finding and identifying the various government agencies that give grants for specific reasons in specific subject areas requires time, effort, and research. Here you will find a good starting point to begin this process.

Again, a great place to look for government grants is the U.S. government's website www.Grants.gov. This site will help you find and apply for the various grant opportunities from all federal agencies.

You can also look for information on the different types of grants and the government agencies that create these grants. Plus, you can sign up to receive instant notification of future grant opportunities in your email inbox.

Furthermore, I again recommend you take a look at the government's Catalog of Federal Domestic Assistance (CFDA), which hosts a complete listing of government grants and other sources of assistance that are available.

Here you will discover information on grants by Category and Topic Area, or you can review the Catalog by searching for various key words (you may find this easier). If you find a particular grant that interests you, make sure that you carefully read the section on Eligibility Requirements. This is essential reading in order to discover if you are eligible and qualified to apply for that particular grant.

You should also know that most grants are not available all year-round. That means that most grants have a cut-off application date. Make sure you pay close attention to these dates before you submit your proposal.

Grants that are offered to individuals can be given for educational support (financial aid), the arts, assistance paying bills, purchasing or fixing up a home, traveling for research and just about anything else you can think of.

If you want to be successful in getting a grant, you certainly should provide the funding agency with a specific plan-of-action that explains your objectives along with a detailed budget.

Whether you apply as an individual or on behalf of your business, a detailed plan-of-action will prove to the organization that you are serious and professional. If given the choice, grant-making organizations (almost without exception) fund people with a detailed well-thought-out PLAN over those that put together unprofessional and unrealistic materials. Especially if the dollar amount of the grant is significant, so do your homework and develop a business plan worth investing in!

If you are awarded a grant you may be required to provide progress reports, program evaluation, and financial reports to the government agency that awarded the grant - so try to be as accurate as possible with your projections.

SMALL BUSINESS GRANT PROPOSALS

This section is going to help you as a small business owner get everything you need in order to give yourself the best chance of receiving the funding you desire.

The next section will be focused on writing a business plan. If you're applying as an individual this section won't necessarily apply to you.

If you're going to be applying for a business grant you'll need to plan out your business ideas and goals so that you can create an effective business plan. It is going to be your business plan that will inevitably decide if you are able to get the funding that you need. You can start by using these tips that will help you to develop your theme for writing the business plan that you will need.

1. You should start by making sure that you clearly define your business idea. Articulate it properly. Know "where you are" and "where you want to be" and how the grant will assist in this plan-of-action.

2. You have to thoroughly examine your motives for getting into the business. Try to convey your passion for this particular business. They want to know "why" you do what you do.

3. Are you realistic? You have to be willing to commit to the hours, discipline, and the frustrations that go along with owning your own business.

4. Conduct a competitive analysis in your market that should include: products, prices, promotions, advertising, distribution, quality, and service. Basically, do you understand your competition? If so, how has this shaped your plan-of-action?

5. You will want to seek out help from other small businesses, vendors, professionals, government agencies, employees, trade associations and trade shows.

PREPARING YOUR BUSINESS PLAN(*IF NEEDED*)

Now that you have a little background on the proper "mind set" required while creating a realistic business plan. We need to move forward and actually CREATE the plan.

At first, it seems like a daunting task. But once you get going you'll find that writing the business plan is not as tough as it seems. You can begin with some of the easy steps first. Some of these are as follows:

Describe your business and what makes it stand out

Talk about the specific market you are targeting

Explain what stage of development your business is currently in - such as, is it brand new or are you buying an up-and-running active business?

If you get hung up on a particular part of the plan, don't worry because you can skip it for now and just come back and fill it in later. You also don't have to worry about making a perfect first draft. Just get some thoughts down on paper to get the process moving forward. You can always come back and "fill in the blanks" later.

STRATEGY IS IMPORTANT

The first half of the business plan is going to be geared towards helping you to develop and support a solid business strategy. This is where you will look at the market, the industry, customers and competitors. Look at your customer needs and ask yourself how your products or services benefit them. What is your competitive advantage… do you have one? What is it that makes you UNIQUE? Plus, you will have to really look at the strengths and weaknesses of each competing business in your area and try to find any opportunities for you and your ideas. All of these steps are largely aimed at helping you create a strategy for your business.

The second half of the business plan is going to be used to execute your selected business strategy. Your products, services, marketing and operations should all closely tie in with your strategy. So while it may be easy for you to choose a well thought out strategy, I would personally recommend you give this a lot of thought. After all, the strategy for your business will set the course for your future.

THINK IN A COMPETITIVE WAY
In today's crowded marketplace, you're probably going to have serious competition no matter how creative and original your business concept may be. That is why you are going to need to think as competitively as possible throughout your entire business plan.

You need to be able to realistically identify where you will do things in a similar manner as your competitors, as well as where you will do things differently. You will want to acknowledge where you have real strengths and where you have real weaknesses.

You should also understand that operating your business significantly better (more efficient, etc) than your competitors may be a very difficult challenge; especially since there are so many of them out there today. Because of this, you are better off if you focus your planning on being different than your competition rather than just on competing with them less directly. For example: Can you find a particular market niche to focus on? Can you find a unique strategy to build your business on?

BE REALISTIC WITH YOUR GOALS

A lot of business plans sound good on paper, but don't work at all when they are used in the real world. As most entrepreneurs understand it can be difficult (sometimes impossible) to attract customers to a new business. Just because you believe in your business plan doesn't mean people are going to become your customers.

People have established buying patterns. While you are trying to bring-in new business, remember, people are "currently" doing business with someone else. In order to win them over, you're going to have to motivate them to make the change with price, quality, service, or convenience ... whatever it takes!

It's also quite possible that when you enter the marketplace, your competitors may react with their own new products, new service, or new lower prices. Furthermore, you need to know that while it's easy to overestimate sales projections it's just as easy to underestimate how much it will cost you to create those projections - especially for a new start-up business.

There are always going to be potential cost overruns, various problems, and overlooked items/issues resulting in more and more expense. With this in mind, you will want to be conservative and try to have extra cash-on-hand tucked away specifically designated for these issues.

OUTLINE OF A COMPLETE BUSINESS PLAN:

Below is exactly what needs to be included in your business plan. This is our quick guide that should be included in ANY business plan:

1. **The executive summary:** The executive summary is what introduces your business strategy to the reader and is the most important section for lending institutions. If you can't convince a grant agency in the first two or three pages that you've got a good business proposal – you're not going to successfully receive any funding.

2. **A small section on company startup:** This section of your business plan is where you have to clearly explain the thought behind the company's creation and how you developed the idea to start your business.

3. **Your company goal:** Use this section to explain what your short and long-term goals are. How fast do you think it will grow? Who will be your primary customers?

4. **Biographies of management:** Define your management team and what they are responsible for and the purposes they serve. Include relevant background, experience, and education.

5. **The product/service you will offer:** What makes your business unique, different, exclusive, and define exactly what product/service you'll bring to the marketplace. What is it that you do?

6. **The market potential:** What is the demand for your product? Is this demand based on needs or wants? Is it a choice? How are you satisfying this demand?

If you're planning to open a locally based business, you need to check out the demand for your offering within a certain radius that is based on what you determine is a reasonable distance from your business. If you are planning to open a Web-based business or one that relies on both the Internet and local traffic for revenues, you'll need to evaluate demand on a local and/or a national basis. You can also seek to get this type of information online as many different sites will perform this analysis for you.

7. **The marketing strategy:** This is the section where you will have to ask yourself how you plan to tell the world you're open for business. For example, questions like: Will you advertise in print, television or on the Web, or all of these? Will you use online marketing tools like search optimization to get your company listed on search engines and advertised on other Web sites? You'll also need to include how much you plan to spend on marketing.

8. **A 3-5 year financial projection:** This section should have a summary of your expected financial forecasts, including spreadsheets showing the method that you used to reach these projections. You'll want to use your balance sheets, income statements, and cash-flow projections for the entire period that year. The summary in this section is also where you would tell grant agencies how much money you'd like to get in order to cover your startup costs. The assumptions that you make in this section will make or break your company's success. If you're unsure about using this kind of financial modeling, find a professional.

SAMPLE BUSINESS PLAN

There is a sample business plan located at
http://www.businesstown.com/planning/creating-rainbow.asp that

follows everything that I covered in the above sections and focuses on a company called "Rainbow Kites, Inc."

SAMPLE SMALL BUSINESS GRANT APPLICATION

When you are looking to get the application process moving forward, you will most likely be a bit anxious to get started. The applications themselves are simple enough. It's mostly the business plan or proposal that is going to require effort on your part.

Applications can be as little as 1 page or many as 15+ pages. Don't let that intimidate you. Just follow the tips below.

PROPOSAL DEVELOPMENT TIPS

The fact of the matter is that you can't avoid writing your proposal. It helps to have some helpful hints that can make the process easier. These tips are not about the writing in the proposal, but more like guidelines that can be used in order to ensure that you follow the entire application process to the letter. Writing the proposal is just one step. You actually have to follow an application procedure to fully develop your proposal. This section will give you some good hints as to how to do that. Let's look at these hints now.

READ AND FOLLOW THE INSTRUCTIONS
Government funding for research purposes is a privilege, not a right. The dates are firm and cannot be changed for any reason; the required forms are necessary; the signatures are necessary. Read the rules and save yourself a lot of irritation later because without following the instructions, you will not get approved.

WRITE CLEARLY
You have to remember that reviewers tend to correlate bad prose with a lack of care and that you are not serious about the process. This

means that if you write poorly, you will not be taken seriously. (If this is an issue, go ahead and hire a professional grant writer.)

HAVE SOMEONE REVIEW YOUR PROPOSAL
You will miss the obvious problems in your proposal because you are too close to them. It is better to have someone that you trust to review your proposal so that you can get an objective opinion.

SPELL AND GRAMMAR CHECK IT
This rule should be obvious, but the reality is that reviewers have a tendency to correlate bad spelling with bad investments. (If this is an issue, go ahead and hire a professional grant writer.)

CLEARLY EXPLAIN WHAT YOU PROPOSE
What you intend to do with the money has to be written as clearly as possible. No guesswork. No questioning. Have someone you trust review your proposal for clarity. The more difficult it is for the reviewer to understand your proposal, the less likely you are going to get approved. So make this process as easy as possible and write with clarity.

KEEP YOUR EYE ON THE BIG PICTURE
This means that you have to place your work in the larger context of your field. You need to able to look ahead and then project what you see to the grant agency.

BE CHARMING
Don't write a grant with a negative tone or attitude. You don't want to cause any unnecessary negativity. You want the reviewers to think of you as an honest and positive person.

USE AN EASY TO READ FONT
You want to make this process as easy on the reviewer as possible. Make sure to use an easy to read font style with an appropriate font size. It must be easy to read.

BASIC HINTS TO KEEP IN MIND:
Keep your text as short as possible. Use short, easy to read sentences.

Clearly state the problem with your finances and your solution. You want to anticipate the questions that you will be asked and answer them.

Credit other people in the field where this would fit. Do not take credit for someone else's ideas.

Do not leave out important information (e.g. budget justifications, vitae, etc) Doing this will make things much more complicated.

Do not inflate the budget to get more money because they will expect this and look for it.

If possible, visit the grant's office to help ensure that all required forms are prepared before the proposal is sent to the funding agency (federal, state, non-profit, corporation, foundation etc…)

Small Business Grants: Review

What's the point in having a great idea if you don't have any cash? You need capital to move your business from an idea to reality. As we've mentioned, one route that you can use to get the money you need is to look for a business grant. Here are some great tips to getting that grant approved.

1) Talk to your local grant agency, local council economic development officer and professional business associations to see if there are any grants available in your specific area.

2) Work out exactly what you need the money for because grants won't be provided for general running costs.

3) Grants are often tied to strict selection criteria such as age, gender, ethnicity, or unemployment and have a specific purpose such as research & development or innovation, training, etc.

4) If possible, try to make personal contact by phone or face to face with the grant's office. Don't send in your application without some type of personal contact. Inform them of your grant request, and see if your idea is a good fit for their organization.

5) Prepare a thorough business plan that stands out from the crowd. Present a thought provoking vision; show a passionate commitment to your plan and a robust cash flow forecast.

6) Grants are often handed out on a cyclical basis. Research upcoming deadlines and be prepared to wait 4-6 weeks and sometimes up to several months for a decision. The larger the amount of money the longer you may have to wait.

7) If you need a large amount of grant money you will (probably) need multiple grants. Go ahead and apply for as many grants as possible. Remember, there is no limit to the amount of grants you can apply for so APPLY!

8) Ask yourself, could this business get up-and-running without grant money? If no one else would invest in it, the grantmaker may be leary of the reasons for such. Look at alternative sources of financing because some funders will require you to be able to match the grant amount.

FUNDRAISING FOR YOUR NON-PROFIT OR ORGANIZATION

Fundraising for your non-profit or community organization follows much the same pattern as a small business grant proposal, but instead of a business plan you will need to include an overview of your organization in your proposal. In responding to a Request for Proposals (RFP) you will also need to effectively present your goals and objectives. Having a well thought out plan of action is important for non-profit grantseekers too. The following is a list of possible sections to include in a grant proposal.

1. Executive Summary: Short summary of the proposal.
2. Organizational Overview/Background Information: Include your organization's mission statement here, along with a brief history of your organization, your programs, structure, and leaders/staff.
3. Statement of Need: State your purpose in applying for grant funds. Provide a compelling reason why your organization should receive support. You may need to present background information on the subject to convey the importance of the situation.
4. Program/Project Description: This is your plan of action. Explain how you will solve the problem – what will be done, who is doing it and how they are qualified, when, and where. Describe the audience and how your project affects them.
5. Goals and Objectives: Describe the desired outcomes of the grant funded activities. List the broad goals of the project and define measurable objectives for each.
6. Methods: How the project will be implemented and evaluated.
7. Budget: Submit a detailed budget; you may want to also include a Budget Narrative for further explanation.
8. Supplementary Materials: You may be required to provide information on the organization's finances, proof of non-profit status, board information and more. As permitted, you may also want to include documents to strengthen your proposal such as staff resumes.

You may also choose to include a cover page and cover letter. Be sure to thoroughly review the grant guidelines and provide all required information.

GRANT TIPS FOR YOUR ORGANIZATION

Pay close attention to submission deadlines and funding level; you don't want to miss a deadline or ask for more funds than are available.

Make your organization shine by listing any similar successfully completed programs or projects – a grant-maker looks for a history of success.

Spotlight the public good that will come from this grant – show how far their grant dollars stretch by illustrating the number of people reached (number of lives changed!) by your organization.

Funders will likely ask you to disclose any financing in place; you may think that if they know about existing funds they won't help, but you can use this to your advantage. Having funding from other sources lends legitimacy to your project. Show them that others have invested in you, but it isn't quite enough to make it happen and this grant can make all the difference!

Keep it going: Funders love it when you demonstrate the ability to use the multiplier effect – for example, a grant will provide training for 5 people, who will then provide training for 25 people, who will then educate the wider community.

Communicate with your grant officer. They are there to help you understand the requirements and answer relevant questions.

INDIVIDUAL GRANT PROPOSALS

Many times individual grant seekers will need to complete an application form, as opposed to writing a grant proposal, but the information requested on the form can be similar to information found in a grant proposal. As demonstrated in the Sample Programs section, there are a wide variety of grants available for individual applicants but you won't be weighed down by the need for a business proposal!

In your search for grants, you may find that many government grants are only available to local governments or organizations. This is the federal government's way of distributing huge amounts of money across the nation. Just look for the award recipients (these can includes states, municipalities, local agencies, and non-profit organizations) and then apply through them directly. However, there are also many programs available only to individuals.

An excellent place to begin your search for individual government grants is http://www.benefits.gov/ -- an official website of the U.S. government. Use the Benefit Finder to determine your eligibility for benefit and assistance programs.

Other professional groups, such as teachers' associations, offer grants for training and teaching materials. Just look around at the groups you may already be involved with for local grant resources – grant money is closer than you think!

WHEN TO USE A GRANT CONSULTANT

Grant consultants and advisors can be an incredibly helpful resource. They can be frauds too. With this in mind, there can be no better ambassador for your cause than you. In the vast majority of cases you will be better off doing everything yourself.

However, there are occasions when grant consultants may be essential for your success. For example, if you're applying for a very large grant and the awarding body is particularly rare and bureaucratic, or the information required needs a technical expertise you do not have, then it can almost be required to appoint a consultant. In most circumstances, however, the cost of consultancy will probably outweigh its usefulness.

Many so-called experts have proved to be nothing more than opportunists! They make false promises so that they can collect fees from clients who have been ultimately left with nothing but a failed grant application.

If you do decide to appoint consultants or advisers check their track record and verify their claims before you make a binding commitment with them.

SUMMARY

As I said earlier, the government is the largest source of "FREE MONEY" and assistance in the world today. And if I had to guess, probably the largest in the history of the world! It doesn't matter if you're poor or rich or middle income – the money is there. Some of these grant applications can be done online. Others need to be completed with good old-fashioned pen & paper and dropped in the mail. Different grants ask for different things and the agencies will answer your questions. Most have websites that are designed to guide you through the process.

Unfortunately, the government doesn't advertise any of this information. They will not tell you what is available unless you know HOW to ask. And even if you do ask, sometimes you may not ask the right question! So you've got to have fun with this. You never know what funders are offering so you must look for yourself. Just know the programs are out there. They are available to you, but you've got to take advantage of them. No one from the government or any other funding institution is going to call you and tell you that you qualify for "this and that"... you have to investigate for yourself. So ask! Again and again and again! After you ASK... you must apply.

So you've got to do a little work, but it's simple. And like just about everything in life – no one can do for you what you must do for yourself.

We've tried to make it as easy as possible.

If you find that you are willing to go through the steps that will be needed in order for you to get your grant, then this will be your guide to making it happen. You are now equipped to not just apply for grants but to receive the grant that you need.

You've learned…

How to look for grant programs to suit your needs

How to apply for them properly

Simple steps to writing a business plan

What to avoid during the grant search and application process

All in all, at this point you have learned enough in order for you to apply for the grant of your choice.

Now…follow the simple steps….and apply for it!

I sincerely hope you enjoyed the information contained in this book, and I thank you for reading.

If you have received value from this book, then I would like to ask you for a favor. Would you be kind enough to leave a review for this book on amazon? I would really appreciate it!

To your success,
~Danielle Green

Made in United States
Orlando, FL
16 October 2023